Foreword by Satoshi Nakamoto

Hello, everyone.

It's been some time since I last shared my thoughts on Bitcoin, and as the world has evolved around it, so has the purpose and understanding of this digital currency. When I created Bitcoin, my aim was simple: to build a system where people could exchange value freely, without borders, and without the need for an intermediary. Bitcoin was born from a vision of independence and trust in a world that sometimes falls short of both.

As Bitcoin has grown beyond what I could have imagined, I've come to appreciate the curiosity and commitment of those who explore it, especially those who seek to understand it for the first time. To each of you who picks up this guide, know that your journey with Bitcoin is just beginning. Approach it with patience, humility, and a long-term view, as all good things take time. Bitcoin's journey has been defined by resilience and growth, and so too should your approach to learning it.

This book distills the essentials of Bitcoin, removing the noise and mystery to get to the heart of what Bitcoin is and why it matters. Remember, Bitcoin isn't a get-rich-quick scheme—it's a tool of empowerment, a gateway to financial freedom, and an invitation to rethink the nature of value itself.

So, read on, explore, and let this guide be your first step into a much larger world. Bitcoin belongs to no one, yet it's a gift for everyone. Take your time, and enjoy the ride.

Best, Satoshi Nakamoto

Preface

Welcome to "Bitcoin Basics: Boring Guide to Understanding Cryptocurrency." When I first stumbled upon Bitcoin in 2017, I was as curious as I was cautious. I had heard the buzz, and seen the headlines, but what drew me in was the idea of a financial system that put people back in control. I didn't dive in with a huge investment. Instead, I started by buying just $1 of Bitcoin a day. Over time, my commitment grew, along with my confidence in the value and potential of cryptocurrency.

This book is written for people just like I was back then—new to Bitcoin, excited but maybe a little overwhelmed. I've distilled everything I've learned into simple, digestible parts.

My goal is to help you understand not just how to buy Bitcoin, but also the mindset that has helped me stay steady, even in a volatile market. Think of this as a guide to take your first steps in the world of cryptocurrency, with strategies and tips to keep you grounded and focused on the long game. Enjoy the journey!

Introduction

If you're reading this, chances are you've heard about Bitcoin and cryptocurrency, but you're wondering where to start. You're not alone. Bitcoin is everywhere in the media stories of massive gains, sudden losses, and everything in between. But beyond the headlines, Bitcoin is a tool that could change the way we think about money and financial independence.

In this book, we'll break down the basics of Bitcoin, the blockchain technology that powers it, and why people are excited about its potential. Whether you're looking to invest, learn the technical side, or just explore this new financial frontier, this guide will walk you through everything you need to know.

This isn't a book about getting rich quickly. Instead, it's a book about steady growth, smart strategies, and an approach to Bitcoin that can fit into any budget or level of risk. We'll go over dollar-cost averaging, a simple way to invest that takes advantage of the ups and downs in Bitcoin's price. We'll also cover the altcoin market-those other cryptocurrencies that often come with higher risk but potentially higher rewards. If you're ready to step into the world of Bitcoin, this book will be your roadmap, guiding you along each part of the journey with clarity and practical advice. So let's get started!

1. Introduction to Bitcoin

Hey there! So, you're curious about Bitcoin. Perfect! Bitcoin is a digital currency that was created to give people financial freedom, without relying on banks. Think of it like money for the internet, but with no middleman, no banks, just peer-to-peer transactions. Let's dive into why Bitcoin's a big deal and how it could change the way we think about money.

2. What is Cryptocurrency?

Cryptocurrency sounds fancy, but it's basically just digital money. It's decentralized, meaning there's no government or central bank controlling it. Instead, it uses blockchain technology—a public ledger that records every transaction securely. This makes it transparent and trustworthy, which is why people are so excited about it.

3. The Birth of Bitcoin

Bitcoin came into existence in 2009, thanks to someone (or a group) called Satoshi Nakamoto. We don't know exactly who they are, which adds to Bitcoin's mystery! Satoshi created Bitcoin as a response to the 2008 financial crisis, wanting a currency that people controlled, not banks. Since then, Bitcoin's journey has been wild-ups, downs, and massive growth in popularity.

4. How Bitcoin Works

Alright, here's where it gets technical, but hang in there! Bitcoin runs on a blockchain. Imagine a digital notebook where every Bitcoin transaction is written down and stored in "blocks." Once a block is filled with transactions, it's linked to the previous block, creating a "chain." Every computer in the network keeps a copy, so it's secure and almost impossible to mess with.

5. Why Use Bitcoin?

Why should you care about Bitcoin? First, it's decentralized, so no single person or government controls it. It's also secure your transactions are private, and Bitcoin can't be easily hacked or counterfeited. For people in countries with unstable currencies or strict financial rules, Bitcoin offers a way to have control over their money.

6. Buying Bitcoin

Okay, so you're ready to buy some Bitcoin! First, you need to set up an account on a cryptocurrency exchange like Coinbase or Binance. Once you're set up, you can buy Bitcoin by linking your bank account or credit card. Just remember, you don't have to buy a whole Bitcoin—you can start with as little as $10 if you want!

7. Storing Bitcoin Safely

Now that you've got Bitcoin, where do you keep it? That's where wallets come in. You have two main options: hot wallets and cold wallets. Hot wallets are connected to the internet (like apps), which makes them convenient but a bit more vulnerable to hackers. Cold wallets, like USB devices, are offline and super secure. If you're holding a lot of Bitcoin, a cold wallet is worth considering.

8. Using Bitcoin in Real Life

Believe it or not, you can actually use Bitcoin to buy stuff! More and more places accept it, from online shops to local businesses. You can also use Bitcoin to transfer money to friends or family around the world. And if you're in it as an investment, you can just hold onto it, hoping it grows in value over time.

9. Risks and Challenges

Bitcoin isn't all sunshine and rainbows. It's still very volatile, meaning its price goes up and down a lot. Some governments are also skeptical about it, and there are scams out there. Always be cautious and don't invest more than you're prepared to lose. But with smart choices, Bitcoin can be a valuable asset.

10. Bitcoin Mining

Ever heard of Bitcoin mining? It's like digital gold mining. Miners use powerful computers to solve complex math problems that help verify transactions. When they solve these problems, they get rewarded with new Bitcoin. But mining isn't easy; it requires a lot of electricity and powerful machines, which makes it less practical for most people these days.

10.5 The Halving: Bitcoin's Built-In Supply Shock

One of the most fascinating aspects of Bitcoin is something called "the halving." Roughly every four years, the number of new Bitcoins mined and released into circulation is cut in half. This process is built into Bitcoin's code to control inflation and limit the total supply to 21 million coins. Think of it like a gradual release valve that gets tighter over time, making Bitcoin more scarce.

Here's why the halving matters: when the supply of new Bitcoin decreases, but demand stays the same (or even increases), it can create a supply shock. This scarcity can often lead to price increases, and historically, each halving has been followed by a significant bull run. This is why some people see the halving as a "fruit-bearing season," a time when Bitcoin's price growth potential is at its peak.

To put it simply, halving events reduce the number of new coins that can be sold by miners. With less Bitcoin hitting the market, each coin can become more valuable. But keep in mind, while previous halvings have led to bull markets, it's not guaranteed to happen every time.

The next halving is a major milestone that many investors watch closely. Understanding the halving is crucial for a long-term strategy; it's a reminder of Bitcoin's finite supply and why holding through the cycles can be rewarding. Just remember: the excitement around the halving can also lead to hype, so stay grounded and remember your strategy. The key here is patience-sometimes the biggest gains come when you least expect them.

11. The Future of Bitcoin

What's next for Bitcoin? Some people think it will become as common as credit cards, while others think it's just a fad. We're seeing new technology, like the Lightning Network, which makes Bitcoin transactions faster and cheaper. No one knows for sure, but one thing's certain—Bitcoin has sparked a global conversation about what money could look like in the future.

12. FAQs and Common Misconceptions

Let's bust a few myths!
Is Bitcoin only for criminals?
Nope. Like any currency, it can be used for good or bad.
Can you lose your Bitcoin?
Yes, if you lose access to your wallet.
Is Bitcoin just a bubble?
Some say yes, but it's been around for over a decade and keeps evolving.
The best approach?
Stay informed and keep learning.

13. Conclusion and Next Steps

Congratulations! You now know the basics of Bitcoin. Whether you're ready to buy, or just want to keep learning, you're on the right track. The world of cryptocurrency is huge and always changing, so take your time exploring. Start small, stay curious, and remember-Bitcoin is about taking control of your financial future.

14. My Personal Strategy

Let me share my personal Bitcoin strategy—it's all about consistency and patience. My approach is long-term dollar-cost averaging (DCA). With DCA, I invest a fixed amount daily, regardless of Bitcoin's price. I started small, buying just $1 a day back in 2017. Over the years, I've grown confident and disciplined in this strategy, and now I'm buying $80 a day, no matter what the market is doing.

Here's why I believe in this approach: Bitcoin's volatility actually works to my advantage. When prices are low, my $80 buys more Bitcoin, letting me accumulate more at a discount. When prices go up, the Bitcoin I've accumulated grows in value, maximizing my gains. Volatility isn't something I fear; instead, I see it as an opportunity to accumulate more when prices dip and benefit when they rise.

I also have a strategy for every four-year cycle, similar to harvesting fruit from a tree. I see Bitcoin as a tree that bears fruit every four years (often tied to Bitcoin's "halving" cycle).

The key is not to cut down the tree, but to pick the fruit when it's ripe. During these cycles, I set a threshold. In this current bull market, I continue to buy my daily $80 of Bitcoin regardless of price. But once my holdings exceed a specific dollar amount—let's say $10,000-anything above that gets sold. So, if my account grows to $12,000, I might sell $2,000 that day or even that hour to lock in profits while keeping a solid base. By doing this, I capture growth while ensuring I don't over-expose myself to risk.

This strategy keeps me focused and steady, allowing me to build my Bitcoin holdings over time and to "harvest" in a way that aligns with the natural cycles of the market.

15. My Altcoin Strategy: Extra Risk, Extra Reward

Now let's talk about my altcoin strategy-where the risks are higher, but the potential rewards can be too. While Bitcoin has been my steady, long-term focus, I've found that many altcoins (alternative cryptocurrencies) can perform even better during market cycles. Some of these coins have their own unique cycles, independent of Bitcoin's, kind of like plants that produce fruit in different seasons. To tap into these opportunities, I buy $1 to $10 a day of various altcoins offered on major exchanges like Coinbase, Robinhood, Gemini, Webull, and Binance.

With altcoins, I follow a similar strategy to my Bitcoin approach: I start slow and stay slow. I don't gamble or rush in, which keeps my risk manageable. When the altcoins begin to "pump" (experience rapid price increases), I take a disciplined approach, selling only what has grown above my set threshold. This way, I capture gains without overexposing myself. It's a way to keep the excitement alive; when prices go up, I'm thrilled with the returns. When prices go down, I'm just as excited because I'm accumulating more at a discount. Now, what if Bitcoin or any other coin goes to zero? Well, in that unlikely event, I'll just keep buying. Imagine the bragging rights of owning all the Bitcoin in the world for $0!

For me, it's about enjoying the journey, adapting to the cycles, and always looking forward to the next opportunity—whatever direction the market takes.

Bonus: Crypto Terms and Sayings for the Newbie Investor

Hey there, future crypto whiz! Here's a quick list of must-know terms and fun sayings you'll hear a lot in the crypto world. Understanding these will keep you in the loop and help you sound like a seasoned trader (or at least help you laugh when you read crypto forums). Let's dive in!

1. FOMO (Fear of Missing Out)
You see Bitcoin or another coin skyrocketing, and you're thinking, "If I don't buy now, I'm going to regret it forever!" Relax. FOMO is real, but remember, slow and steady wins the race.

2. HODL
Originally a typo for "hold," this now means "Hold On for Dear Life." If you HODL, you're keeping your coins through thick and thin, ignoring the crazy ups and downs. HODLers believe in the long game.

3. Whale
A big player with a lot of Bitcoin or other coins who can move the market. When a whale buys or sells, prices can go nuts. Watch out for those splashes!

4. DYOR (Do Your Own Research)
Basically, "don't just take my word for it." This is your reminder to look things up yourself before you invest, no matter how good it sounds.

5. To the Moon
When people say a coin is going "to the moon," they mean they think it's about to skyrocket in value. Get ready for some &, emojis!

6. Shill
When someone promotes a coin endlessly, hoping others will buy and drive the price up. Be cautious of shills—they usually have their own agenda.

7. FUD (Fear, Uncertainty, and Doubt)
When negative rumors are spread to cause panic and drive prices down. Ignore the FUD and remember your strategy!

8. Bagholder
Someone who bought in at a high price and is now "holding the bag" as the value drops. We've all been there. The key? Patience.

9. Pump and Dump
When a coin's price is artificially pumped up so people can sell at a profit, then it crashes. Don't get caught chasing these pumps; they're short-lived.

10. Altcoin
Any coin that isn't Bitcoin. There are thousands of them, and each one has a community that thinks it's the next big thing.

11. WAGMI (We're All Gonna Make It)

A saying to spread positivity and remind everyone in the community that good things are coming. Keep the faith and enjoy the journey!

12. Sats (Satoshis)

The smallest unit of Bitcoin, named after Bitcoin's creator, Satoshi Nakamoto. One Bitcoin is made up of 100 million "sats." So, even if you can't buy a whole Bitcoin, you can still stack sats!

13. Ape In

To buy into a coin aggressively without much research. Sometimes it works out, but other times..well, let's just say apes don't always make the best financial decisions.

14. Rekt

When you lose big in a trade.
As in, "I bought the top, and now I'm totally rekt." Don't worry, even the pros get rekt sometimes.
It's all part of the game.

15. Paper Hands vs. Diamond Hands

Paper Hands: Someone who sells at the first sign of trouble. Diamond Hands: Someone who holds on, no matter what, confident in their investment. Decide which hands you want to have!

Bonus: Helpful Resources for Your Crypto Journey

Alright, now that you've got the basics, let's make sure you have some powerful tools at your fingertips. Here's a list of go-to websites and resources that can help you stay informed, track your investments, and make smarter decisions. These are some of the most popular sites in the crypto community, and trust me—they'll be your new best friends!

1. CoinMarketCap [coinbasecap.com]
The ultimate place to track prices, market cap, and rankings for thousands of cryptocurrencies. You can also check each coin's historical performance, news, and upcoming events. If you're starting out, this is a must-have bookmark.

2. Crypto Bubbles [cryptobubbles.net]
A fun and visual way to see the market's performance. Each bubble represents a coin, growing or shrinking based on its price change. It's a great way to get a snapshot of what's going on in the market at a glance. Plus, it's kind of addictive!

3. CoinGecko [coingecko.com]
An alternative to CoinMarketCap with some unique features. CoinGecko ranks coins and provides tons of extra data, like developer activity and social media engagement. Great for research!

4. Binance Academy [academy.binance.com]
Free educational content covering everything from beginner to advanced topics. Whether you're learning about blockchain basics or diving into technical analysis, Binance Academy has you covered with clear, easy-to-follow lessons.

5. TradingView [tradingview.com]
A powerful charting tool for tracking crypto (and other assets) in detail. You can customize indicators, set up alerts, and view in-depth charts. Perfect for anyone interested in learning technical analysis.

6. Glassnode [glassnode.com]
An on-chain data platform that gives you insights into the health and activity of the blockchain itself. See metrics like wallet activity, network health, and transaction volume. Some features are free, and it's great for getting a deeper understanding of the crypto market.

7. CryptoPanic [cryptopanic.com]
A news aggregator for all things crypto. Keep up with the latest headlines, social media mentions, and market-moving news. You can also filter by positive or negative sentiment to get a quick sense of the market mood.

8. Messari [messari.io]

An in-depth research platform that offers news, analysis, and insights. It's a bit more advanced, but if you're serious about understanding the market fundamentals, Messari is a top choice.

9. Subreddit r/Cryptocurrency [reddit.com/r/CryptoCurrency]

One of the most popular forums for discussing all things crypto. From breaking news to meme culture, Reddit is where a lot of the crypto community hangs out. It's a great place to learn from others, ask questions, and stay in the loop.

10. CoinDesk [coindesk.com]

One of the most trusted news sources in crypto. CoinDesk covers news, analysis, and major events in the cryptocurrency and blockchain world.

Bookmark this if you want to stay informed without getting overwhelmed. Whether you're checking prices, reading up on the latest news, or exploring deep data, these resources will help keep you in the know. The crypto world moves fast, so having these tools on hand can make all the difference as you navigate the highs and lows.

Happy learning!

Bonus: My Favorite Crypto YouTuber & Course Teacher

If there's one person who stands out in the crypto space for being a true guide, it's Steve from Crypto Crew University. Steve isn't just another YouTuber—he's like the wise friend you wish you had when you first got into crypto. He's known for his no-nonsense, fact-based approach, going against the herd and keeping it real when everyone else is hyping up the market.

Steve has this amazing ability to call the major bottoms and tops of the market. It's uncanny! He's one of the few out there who can see the big picture and stay cool, calm, and collected when the market is full of hype or panic. And he's not just in it for the fame or the sponsorships—Steve actually refuses them. He's a humble, family-oriented guy who genuinely wants to help his viewers make the best decisions.

Watching Steve is like getting advice from that wise family member who's been through it all and just wants to see you succeed.
If you're looking to follow someone who "spits facts" and provides real value, Steve from Crypto Crew University is the go-to. He's helped thousands of people with his insight and strategies, not by jumping on trends but by staying grounded and focusing on what really matters. So if you want to learn from someone who's all about true value, humility, and real love for the crypto community, check him out—

You won't regret it!

Final Thoughts: Be Smart, Stay Steady

As we wrap up, here's one last message from me to you— stay cautious, stay smart, and don't get swept up by the hype. The crypto world can be exciting, but remember: the moments when everyone's celebrating new all-time highs are often the times to be most careful. When the market is euphoric, prices tend to be inflated, and seasoned investors often wait to sell to eager newcomers, leaving them "holding the bag" as prices come back down. Don't be the liquidity for these experienced players.

If you're buying, especially at high points, go slow. Buy in tiny amounts if you're curious, just enough to learn without over-committing. Remember, in crypto, the real opportunities often come during quiet times, not during the frenzied peaks. The best way to succeed is by being patient, steady, and avoiding impulsive moves.

This isn't a race, and you don't need to "make it big" overnight. Focus on learning, growing, and having fun with the process. Crypto is a journey that rewards those who take their time, build knowledge, and stay cautious, especially when others are chasing the hype. Don't give your hard-earned money away to the more experienced investors who know how to navigate these ups and downs.

Stay safe, stay grounded, and remember—you're in control. Take your time, and let crypto be something that adds value to your life, not stress.

Thank you for reading, and here's to a smart, steady, and successful journey ahead!

www.ingramcontent.com/pod-product-compliance
Lightning Source LLC
Chambersburg PA
CBHW050328220526
45465CB00005B/2176